Discovering

a

Forgiveness

Plan

Discovering a Forgiveness Plan

melody carlson

by design book 4

TH1NK Books
an imprint of NavPress®

TH1NK
P.O. Box 35001
Colorado Springs, Colorado 80935

ISBN 1-57683-728-9

Cover design by Disciple Design
Illustration: Collins Dillard, Disciple Design
Creative Team: Gabe Filkey (s.c.m.), Karen Lee-Thorp, Darla Hightower, Arvid Wallen, Glynese Northam

Published in association with the literary agency of Sara A. Fortenberry.

Printed in Canada

1 2 3 4 5 6 7 8 9 10 / 09 08 07 06 05

FOR A FREE CATALOG OF
NAVPRESS BOOKS & BIBLE STUDIES,
CALL 1-800-366-7788 (USA)
OR 1-800-839-4769 (CANADA)

contents

introduction

*N*o one on this planet can escape the need to forgive—or to be forgiven. Yet forgiveness can be so hard to put into practice at times. Seriously, the last thing you want to do is to forgive that jerk who hurt you so deeply. You know she doesn't deserve it. Sure, maybe you'd like to forget that the incident ever happened, but you have absolutely no desire to forgive. At least not right now.

Do you know that some people will spend their entire lives in a state of bitterness—all because they never learned to forgive? But what they don't realize is that they have locked themselves into an invisible prison, and they wound themselves far more than they ever harm the ones they refuse to forgive.

That's not God's plan for your life. God knows how desperately you need forgiveness. *Discovering a Forgiveness Plan* is your guide to understanding God's design for your life when it comes to not only receiving God's forgiveness but forgiving yourself and others as well.

about this series

*T*he *By Design* series was created to help you experience God's Word in a fun, fresh, and personal way. *Knowing God Better Than Ever* is a great book to start with since it's pretty basic and foundational. The topics of the other three books—*Finding Out Who You Really Are, Making the Most of Your Relationships,* and *Discovering a Forgiveness Plan*—were selected for how they specifically relate to what's going on in your life and can be used in any order that appeals to you.

how to use this book

*T*here are a couple of ways to use this book. You can do it with a group or on your own, whichever works best for you. But sometimes it's easier to stick with something when you do it with friends. And it can be more fun too. If that's the case, you should pick a specific day and time when you'll meet (once a week) to go over that week's chapter together. You should also decide who will take the role of group leader (this helps to keep things rolling in the right direction).

And, naturally, everyone should read and do the writing assignments before getting together. Then when you meet, you can go over the chapter, share your answers or questions, things you've learned, goals you've made, goals you've attained, or goals you've blown (no one's perfect). And always make sure that you pray for each other during the week. After six weeks, you will not only have completed this Bible study book, but you'll feel a lot closer to your friends too.

As you go through each week's chapter, you can decide what pace works best for you. Some will want to read just a few pages each day, taking time to soak it in and carefully complete the assignments. Others may prefer to do one whole chapter at a sitting — but if that's the case, make sure you go back over it during the rest of the week (consider the Bible verses or goals you've made).

Mostly, you need to discover which way works best for you and then stick with it. And hopefully, as you work through this series, you'll appreciate how God's Word really does have meaning and practical guidance for your life.

the master
plan

If . . . my people, my God-defined people,

respond by humbling themselves,

praying, seeking my presence,

and turning their backs on their wicked lives,

I'll be there ready for you:

I'll listen from heaven,

forgive their sins,

and restore their land to health.

2 Chronicles 7:14

orgiveness takes center stage in Christianity. It's probably one of the first things you heard about as a new Christian. Yet so many Christians just don't get it. Or maybe they just don't *give* it.

Okay, so now you're wondering—what exactly is *forgiveness* anyway? In a nutshell, forgiveness is the conscious choice to overlook it when someone hurts you. It means that even though you've been offended, you don't hold it against that person—you let it go and move on. Now that might sound fairly simple, but it's one of those things that's a lot easier said than done.

God knew right from the start that mankind would need forgiveness. He knew that because he created us to be *human* and, unlike the animal kingdom, we were given the ability to make moral choices. Meaning you get to decide what you'll do—whether it's good, bad, or ugly—it's your choice. And God knew that, as humans, we would make some very bad choices, and consequently we would hurt others and ourselves and, as a result, *we* would need to be forgiven.

Sounds pretty straightforward, right? Sure, if you were really wise and if you totally understood and accepted God's plan for forgiveness, you would get this. But instead you are human and subject to making mistakes, and sometimes (like the rest of the human race) you like to learn things the hard way. God knew this too. After all, he is God.

So to really understand God's forgiveness plan, you need to go back to the beginning of time. And since you don't have a time machine, your main tool must be the Bible, specifically, the book of Genesis, but for now let's use the nutshell version.

In the beginning, when God created the world and everything in it, he made man "in his image" (meaning mankind had the ability to reason, to make decisions, to rule over the animals, stuff like that). That's where Adam and Eve and the Garden of Eden came in. God loved his human creation and really wanted life to be good for them, so he gave them everything they needed (and according to history and geography, the Garden of Eden really was a "paradise" with warm weather and delicious edible vegetation like grapes, pomegranates, figs, melons, apples—not unlike a really good day in Maui). Even so, Adam and Eve chose to do the one thing God had told them *not* to do. In other words, they made a bad decision and the rest of mankind has been following this example ever since.

But God—being loving, kind, patient—decided that he didn't want to allow sin to come between him and the humans he loved—and that's why he designed a way for us to be forgiven and reconnected with him.

for·give [for giv), v., -gave, -giv·en, -giv·ing. –v.t.

1. to grant pardon for or remission of (an offense, sin, etc.); absolve. 2. to cancel or remit (a debt, obligation, etc.). 3. to grant pardon to (a person). 4. to cease to feel resentment against: *to forgive one's enemies.* –v.i. 5. to pardon an offense or an offender. [bef. 900; ME, OE *forgiefan]* —**for·giv·able,** *adj.* –**for·giv·er,** *n.* –**Syn.** See EXCUSE

(from *Random House Webster's College Dictionary* © 1997.)

After the First Sin

When they heard the sound of GOD strolling in the garden
in the evening breeze, the Man and his Wife hid in the
trees of the garden, hid from GOD.
GOD called to the Man: "Where are you?"
He said, "I heard you in the garden and I was afraid
because I was naked. And I hid."
GOD said, "Who told you you were naked?
Did you eat from that tree I told you not to eat from?"
The Man said, "The Woman you gave me as a companion,
she gave me fruit from the tree, and, yes, I ate it."
Genesis 3:8-12

What About This?

1. Adam and Eve were embarrassed after they sinned. Describe a time when you chose to disobey God.

2. How would you feel if you knew God was watching you at that particular moment? What would you say to him?

3. Why do you think Adam immediately blamed Eve for the fact that he blew it?

After All I've Done . . .

Later in the Old Testament, through a series of events, God's people wind up as slaves in Egypt. But once again, God has mercy on them and sends Moses to help them escape their captors. To accomplish this, God does amazing miracles (like raining zillions of frogs from the sky, turning the river to blood, parting the Red Sea), and later on he even provides them with food and water as they travel through the desert. Even so, the people complain, they don't trust Moses' leadership, and finally when they are at the border of their destination (the Promised Land) they completely lose it. Caving to fear, they refuse to enter the Land of Milk and Honey.

Well, if you were God, you'd probably be totally fed up with these whiners by then—maybe you would've even utilized your superpowers and simply zapped them off the planet altogether. But when Moses pleaded with God to forgive them, God agreed. However, God didn't allow the people who had doubted him to go into the Promised Land. Even God has to draw the line sometimes.

"Please forgive the wrongdoing of this people out of the extravagance of your loyal love just as all along, from the time they left Egypt, you have been forgiving this people."

God said, "I forgive them, honoring your words.
But as I live and as the Glory of God fills the whole Earth—
not a single person of those who saw my Glory,
saw the miracle signs I did in Egypt and the wilderness,
and who have tested me over and over and over again,
turning a deaf ear to me—
not one of them will set eyes on the land I so solemnly
promised to their ancestors.
No one who has treated me with such repeated contempt
will see it."

Numbers 14:19-23

What Do You Think?

4. List three cool things that you believe God has done for you.

5. Describe an incident when you doubted God.

6. What did your doubt cause you to do?

maggie's story

I've been a Christian for most of my life, and it's not like I'm ready to toss it exactly, but I am seriously questioning whether or not it's worth it. I mean, I try to do things right (I go to Bible study and church and youth group), and I try to be a good, caring, sensitive kind of person, but it seems like life just keeps going sideways on me. And no matter how hard I pray about certain things, the situation just keeps getting worse. And sometimes, like today, I feel totally fed up with God!

It's about my parents. Up until this year, I thought I had one of the few "original" sets of parents. I mean, seriously, most of my friends' parents have already separated, divorced, remarried — and some have done it more than once. Okay, it's not like my parents are perfect, they've always had their fair share of fights, but somehow I never thought they would totally throw in the towel — especially since they're both supposedly Christians and have gone to church for as long as I can remember. But as it turns out, I was dead wrong.

The pathetic thing is that I was actually feeling hopeful when I went to youth group last night. My parents pleasantly told me that they were going to spend the evening together "to discuss some things," and in order to give them more time and privacy, I decided to spend the night at my best friend, Claire's, house after youth group. Not only that but Claire and I even spent some time praying for my parents before we went to bed!

Like that really worked!

So today I come home feeling all hopeful and positive only to discover that my dad has left us. "What do you mean, he's left us?" I ask my mom after she informs me of this new development.

"Sit down, Maggie," she says in a voice that doesn't sound quite natural.

"I don't want to sit down." I drop my backpack on the kitchen floor, fold my arms across my chest and just stand there, waiting.

"Fine." She takes in a deep breath, then gets this look like she's getting ready to recite some rehearsed piece that she's been working on just for me. "Your dad and I have decided that it's better for him to live somewhere else for the time being."

"Somewhere else?" I press my lips tightly together and study her. I'm trying to keep from saying something really mean, something I'll be sorry for, but the truth is, I'm pretty certain that she's the problem. I suspect that she lost her cool and threw him out last night.

"He's staying at Gary's for a few days . . . " she says, "until he finds something more permanent."

"Permanent?" I hear the pitch of my voice get higher. "I thought you said for the time being? Now you're saying permanent? What's up, Mom? What did you do to drive him away?"

My mom looks hurt by this, but she doesn't answer me. She just meticulously gathers up a newspaper that's spread across the breakfast bar and neatly stacks it together as if this is the most important thing in the world.

"Why?" I demand. "Why can't you guys work this thing out? I thought you were Christians, and I thought that Christians weren't supposed to get divorced. Didn't you guys make a promise to God when you got married? Didn't you say 'until death do we part'? Well, nobody died yet, did they?"

"Maggie — " Mom gives me that you-can't-understand-this-because-you're-only-sixteen-look.

"Did they?" I persist. "Did someone die?"

"Oh, Maggie. Please, don't make this any harder than it already is."

"Harder for who? Looks like you don't have it too hard, Mom. You're still here in the house. Dad's the one who got thrown out — he's the one who has to go stay someplace else. You should be happy now, Mom — you've practically got the whole house to yourself! You won't have to complain about Dad leaving his running shoes in the den anymore." I grab her neat stack of newspapers and throw it into the air. "Or his newspapers littered all over the place." Then I grab my backpack and storm out the door, get into my car, slam the door, and take off.

I am so angry that I can hardly see to drive. Or maybe it's those stupid tears pouring down my face that are messing with my vision. Okay, I know that I was really awful to Mom, but then she's been even worse to my dad — so horrible that she's finally driven him away! And it totally infuriates me. But I'm not just mad at Mom right now. I'm mad at God too. They've both let me down!

> Help, GOD—the bottom has fallen out of my life!
> Master, hear my cry for help!
> Listen hard! Open your ears!
> Listen to my cries for mercy.
> If you, GOD, kept records on wrongdoings,
> who would stand a chance?
> As it turns out, forgiveness is your habit,
> and that's why you're worshiped.
>
> Psalm 130:1-4

What About You?

7. Maggie is angry at God. Like the writer of Psalm 130, she feels like the bottom has dropped out of her life. Have you ever felt like this? Describe the incident.

8. What did, or would, you do if you felt this angry at God or someone else?

A Sneak Preview . . .

In the Old Testament, God offered his people a means of making things right between them and himself—it was called *sacrificing*. People would bring something of value (like farm animals) to sacrifice to God as a way of asking for forgiveness. Perhaps this was God's way of reminding them of the seriousness of their sins, because it forced them to witness the bloodshed of innocent animals and realize that this was being done to restore their relationship with God.

One time God asked for a different kind of sacrifice. Abraham had already proven his devotion to God by leaving his homeland and heading out to the wilderness after God told him to go. God had promised Abraham that he would be the "father of nations" even though he and his wife were elderly and childless. So you can imagine Abraham's joy when God fulfilled his promise by miraculously giving them a son—Isaac. Then later on, when Isaac was a young man, God asked Abraham to offer this son as a sacrifice—meaning Abraham was supposed to kill him.

So Abraham faithfully took Isaac to the appointed place and actually sharpened his knife, getting ready to sacrifice his beloved son, but God intervened and sent a wild ram to take Isaac's place on the altar. Even so, you can imagine how this scene must've gotten Abraham's full attention. This story was told generation after generation, until one day, thousands of years later, it was reenacted in a far more dramatic way—a way that would change the history of the world and forgiveness for eternity.

The angel of God spoke from Heaven a second time to Abraham:
"I swear—God's sure word!—because you have gone through with this,
and have not refused to give me your son, your dear, dear son,
I'll bless you—oh, how I'll bless you!
And I'll make sure that your children flourish—
like stars in the sky! like sand on the beaches!
And your descendants will defeat their enemies.
All nations on Earth will find themselves blessed through
your descendants because you obeyed me."

Genesis 22:15-18

Getting Honest

So, answer these questions:

9. Different people tend to see God from different viewpoints. Some perceive him as a stern judge; others view him as a loving father. Describe how you see him.

10. In your own words, define the word forgiveness.

11. Do you believe that you need God's forgiveness? Why or why not?

12. How does it feel to be forgiven? Describe a time when you experienced forgiveness.

13. Do you think God really has forgiven you? Why or why not?

Why It Didn't Work

If you read through the entire Old Testament, you might be amazed at how often God's chosen people totally blew it. Again and again, they turned their backs on God, they forgot his blessings and broke his commandments, they doubted, they rebelled, and occasionally they repented. And every time they repented, God faithfully forgave them. But somehow they moved further and further away from God.

By the end of Old Testament times, some of God's people noticed this problem. But the solution they came up with only made things worse. They decided to elaborate on God's commandments with rules and restrictions about the right and wrong ways to live. So they filled books with thousands of convoluted rules—many as ridiculous as calling it "sinful" if someone carried anything heavier than a hard-boiled egg on the Sabbath.

So instead of focusing on loving God and each other, they were distracted by rules and trying to gain God's favor and forgiveness through their own means. The problem was that these man-made rules and restrictions gave people a false sense of forgiveness—they were convinced that their devotion to this Law was all it took please God and remain in his favor. But what God really wanted from them was *devotion to him*. He wanted his people to love him—with "all their hearts, minds, and souls." He wanted a close and intimate relationship with them, where they would repent to him and he would offer forgiveness on his own terms. But their Law consistently pulled them away from him—until finally God knew it was time to implement Part Two of his divine forgiveness plan.

Ask Yourself . . .

14. Do I think that if I "obey" all the rules (like meeting curfew or making my bed) that I won't need God's forgiveness? Why or why not?

15. What motivates me to go to God to be forgiven? Explain.

16. Why does God care so much about forgiveness? Why doesn't he just lower the standard to something I can handle?

The Promise

"This is the brand-new covenant that I will make with
Israel when the time comes.
I will put my law within them—write it on their hearts!—
and be their God.
And they will be my people.
They will no longer go around setting up schools to teach
each other about God.
They'll know me firsthand, the dull and the bright, the smart and the slow.
I'll wipe the slate clean for each of them. I'll forget they ever sinned!"
GOD's Decree.
Jeremiah 31:33-34

word puzzle

Just for fun—see if you can write one word (for each letter of the word forgiveness) that represents an area of your life where you might need forgiveness (past, present, or future).

F

O

R

G

I

V

E

N

E

S

S

Words to Live By

(Consider memorizing one of these.)

He forgives your sins—every one.

He heals your diseases—every one.

He redeems you from hell—saves your life!

He crowns you with love and mercy—a paradise crown.

He wraps you in goodness—beauty eternal.

He renews your youth—you're always young in his presence.

Psalm 103:3-5

GOD, you smiled on your good earth!

You brought good times back to Jacob!

You lifted the cloud of guilt from your people,

you put their sins far out of sight.

You took back your sin-provoked threats,

you cooled your hot, righteous anger.

Psalm 85:1-3

Journal Your Thoughts

Choose one of the verses above. Write below what those words mean to you.

My Goal

You're starting to learn about God's master plan for forgiveness. But the purpose of this Bible study is to challenge you to work on the design of your life. So consider one or two goals that you'd like to write in regard to God's forgiveness plan for you. (Examples: *I want to accept God's forgiveness for me*, or *I want to better understand forgiveness*.)

My Goal(s):

My Prayer

Use this space to write a prayer. You can ask God to help you fulfill your goals, or to show you if there's someone you need to forgive, or to help you to receive his forgiveness. Just write a prayer that comes straight from your heart!

You're my God; have mercy on me.
I count on you from morning to night.
Give your servant a happy life;
I put myself in your hands!
You're well-known as good and forgiving,
bighearted to all who ask for help.
Pay attention, God, to my prayer;
bend down and listen to my cry for help.

Psalm 86:3-6

the intervention
plan

This is how much God loved the world:

He gave his Son, his one and only Son.

And this is why: so that no one need be destroyed;

by believing in him, anyone can have a whole and lasting life.

God didn't go to all the trouble of sending his Son

merely to point an accusing finger,

telling the world how bad it was.

He came to help,

to put the world right again.

John 3:16-17

*N*ow we come to Part Two of God's forgiveness plan — this is the part where hope enters. The Old Testament rules weren't really working, meaning they didn't do much to draw God and mankind back together again. If anything, the gulf was growing wider with each generation. But God had a plan to bridge this chasm.

Imagine for a moment that you own a large corporation in, say, Melbourne, Australia, but you live in New York City. And suppose your corporation is having some problems, like production is way down and the work is shoddy and your employees are stealing the profits and you're worried about going bankrupt. What do you do? Most likely you'd get on a plane and get down there to see what could be done to straighten things out. Maybe you'd even do it incognito (disguised as a worker) so that you could really see what was going on and hopefully do something to remedy the problems.

That's sort of like what God decided to do. He decided to become "one of us" by miraculously pouring himself into the form of a helpless human baby that was born of a human woman — and as you've probably guessed, that baby's name was Jesus Christ, and he is the Son of God. And Jesus lived among the human race and experienced all the things that humans experience. And eventually he began a ministry to teach everyone about God and how much God loved everyone. And people listened. And they watched him perform all sorts of miracles. And they began to believe that he really was the Son of God. But the religious leaders weren't ready to say good-bye to their old "rules and regulations," so jealous of Jesus' ministry and his following, they saw to it that he was brutally beaten and killed. End of story.

Well, not actually. The thing is, God knew this was going to happen — it was part of his plan. He'd even shown this very thing to godly men thousands of years earlier — these were the prophets (like Isaiah and Jeremiah) who wrote about Jesus (the Messiah) in the Old Testament. And when Jesus died on the cross, he was the final sacrifice — the only sacrifice that would, once and for all, offer forgiveness to everyone. In other words, Jesus was the bridge of forgiveness that spanned the gulf between God and the human race. His death on the cross is your ticket to God's forgiveness and love.

The New Deal

I want you to know, my very dear friends,
that it is on account of this resurrected Jesus
that the forgiveness of your sins can be promised.
He accomplishes, in those who believe,
everything that the Law of Moses could never make good on.
But everyone who believes in this raised-up Jesus
is declared good and right and whole before God.

Acts 13:38-39

What About This?

1. Acts says, "It is on account of this resurrected Jesus that the forgiveness of your sins can be promised." Do you believe this? If so, what's the connection between his resurrection and forgiveness? If not, what are the roadblocks for you?

2. Describe how you feel when you consider that Jesus died a brutal death, was nailed to a cross—for you.

3. Have you consciously accepted Jesus' forgiveness? Why or why not?

4. Why do you think God felt this was the best way to forgive everyone?

Clean Slate

If you've ever blown it (and if you're human, you probably have), you know how good it feels to get a fresh start. Say it's midterm and you realize that you haven't been keeping up in geometry and, consequently, your grade is in the toilet and it's really going to mess up your GPA, which you've been trying to keep up so that your car insurance rates will go down . . . but now it's too late. Well, what if your geometry teacher said, "Okay, this one time, I'm scrapping the grades—you get a second chance to improve your grade during the second half of the term"? While that will probably never happen in real life, wouldn't it feel pretty great? Wouldn't you be totally relieved?

That's a little like the power of forgiveness—it's like taking a shower after you've been covered in mud, or having someone clean your room after the junk has really piled up, or getting a makeover that makes you want to start over—it's like a fresh start, a clean slate, a second chance, and it feels pretty good. And when Jesus forgives you, it's even better!

> When you were stuck in your old sin-dead life,
> you were incapable of responding to God.
> God brought you alive—right along with Christ!
> Think of it! All sins forgiven,
> the slate wiped clean,
> that old arrest warrant canceled
> and nailed to Christ's Cross.
> Colossians 2:13-14

What About You?

5. Have you ever been stuck, cornered, like you had nowhere to turn? Describe the situation and how you felt.

6. Now describe how you felt when you realized there was a way out. Or how you felt if there wasn't.

maggie's story continues

Before I get in a wreck, I finally come to my senses and pull over. I take out my cell phone and call Claire.

"Can I crash at your house for a while?" I ask.

"Sure," she says, sounding worried. "What's wrong?"

"My parents."

"Are they fighting again?"

"No. It's worse. I'll tell you when I get there."

So I dry my eyes and drive over to Claire's and dump the whole ugly story on her. I know she understands since her parents split up when she was about ten. Of course, both her mom and dad have remarried since then, and both of them seem relatively happy in their new marriages, at least most of the time, but Claire still feels torn between the two sets of parents.

"That's too bad," she says when I finally finish. "I really thought they were going to stick it out."

"Me too."

"You really think it's all your mom's fault?"

I nod. "She's constantly been on his case lately, always nagging him to do something or other — and even when he tries, it's like it's never good enough for her. And then they get into a big old fight. I'm sure that's what happened last night while I was gone. And I bet Dad got fed up, like he just couldn't take it anymore. So he left."

"Which one do you think you'll live with?"

Now I hadn't actually considered this. I mean, I figure I'll stay in our house, since that's where my room is and everything, but I guess if my dad got a place of his own, and if it was nearby . . .

"I don't know," I finally admit. "Right now, I'd rather be with Dad. I'm so furious at Mom. It's like this is totally her fault. If she'd just be nicer or more patient. I can't believe she thinks she's a Christian."

"Even Christians blow it, Maggie."

I roll my eyes at her. "Duh."

"Have you talked to your dad yet?"

I shake my head no. "I was thinking of calling him, but I wanted to wait until I cooled off, you know. It's like I needed some space to think."

"Well, you can stay here as long as you like. Mom and Doug drove over to Sprague to see Meredith's new baby."

"And you didn't want to see your new little nephew?" I tease, since I know she doesn't like people to assume that Meredith is her sister just because she's Doug's daughter. It doesn't help matters that Meredith treats Claire like dirt.

"I'll be nice to the baby," says Claire, "and little Ian can even call me Aunt Claire if he wants, but that's as far as it goes."

"Man, what if my parents get remarried," I suddenly say. "And what if I get stuck with stupid stepsisters and brothers too?"

"Speaking of siblings, has anyone told Brianna yet?"

Brianna's my older sister, a sophomore in college, and fully aware of our parents' recent marital difficulties. "I haven't e-mailed her yet, but I'm sure that Mom has informed her by now—of course, Mom probably made it sound like she was Ms. Innocent and that the whole thing is Dad's fault."

"Is that how she acted to you?"

Now I consider this. "Not exactly."

"Maybe you should get both sides of the story, Maggie."

"Yeah. I guess I should call Dad and see how he's doing." So I take out my cell and speed dial his number. While I'm at it, I think I'll even bring up the possibility of living with him, when he gets a place, instead of Mom. That might actually make Dad feel better about all this too.

If we claim that we're free of sin, we're only fooling ourselves.

A claim like that is errant nonsense.

On the other hand, if we admit our sins—make a clean breast of them—

he won't let us down; he'll be true to himself.

He'll forgive our sins and purge us of all wrongdoing.

If we claim that we've never sinned, we out-and-out contradict God—

make a liar out of him.

A claim like that only shows off our ignorance of God.

1 John 1:8-10

What About That?

7. Describe how you think Maggie is feeling now. Why does she feel like that?

8. What do you think 1 John 1:9 means when it says, "If we admit our sins . . . He'll forgive our sins"?

9. Have you ever admitted your sins to God? If so, how did you feel before you did it? How did you feel afterward? Or, if you've never admitted your sins to God, what's holding you back?

A Two-Way Street

So does this mean that God's forgiveness hinges on whether or not you are willing to confess your sins to him? Like you can't have one without the other? And if so, what's up with that? Can't God just be nice and forgive you and get on with it?

Okay, what if your best friend did something that deeply hurt you? Sure, it's possible that you might be able to forgive her without actually having a conversation, but would your relationship really be the same as before? Wouldn't it be better if she was honest with you, admitting that she did something really raunchy, something that she's really sorry for—and *then* you forgave her? Of course!

And it's the same way with God. He wants you to be honest with him, to express your heartfelt regret and to see that you've blown it. Not only does it repair your relationship with him but hopefully you learn from it and don't make the same mistake again.

Count yourself lucky, how happy you must be—
you get a fresh start,
your slate's wiped clean.
Count yourself lucky—
GOD holds nothing against you
and you're holding nothing back from him.
Psalm 32:1-2

what's your HQ?

HQ stands for honesty quotient. How honest are you with yourself, others, and most importantly, God? Now, be honest as you rate the following fifteen statements.

Answers: A = Often, B = Sometimes, C = Never

circle one

1. If a good friend gets a bad haircut, I still tell her it's cute.

   A   B   C

2. I see a dollar on the floor and pocket it. Finders, keepers.

   A   B   C

3. I'm very concerned about what other people think of me.

   A   B   C

4. During a test, I accidentally see someone's answer and use it.

   A   B   C

5. If I'm late for class, I think it's okay to make up a good excuse. A   B   C

6. If no one notices that I get home after curfew, I don't mention it.

   A   B   C

7. I pretend to like a movie if my friends really like it.

   A   B   C

8. I don't like to admit to doing something wrong.

   A   B   C

9. What people don't know won't hurt them.

   A   B   C

10. It's okay to copy things from the Internet to use in my report.

    A   B   C

11. I like appearing to be a strong Christian at youth group.

    A   B   C

12. I would cheat if I knew I wouldn't be caught.

    A   B   C

13. When telling an exciting incident, I tend to exaggerate.

    A   B   C

14. I like to say what I think other people want to hear.

    A   B   C

15. While praying, I skim over anything that's negative about me.

    A   B   C

A answers = 1 point each

B answers = 3 points each

C answers = 10 points each

Now add up your answers and see what your HQ really is.

15–30 = Liar, Liar, Pants on Fire. Your HQ and your integrity are seriously at risk. Ask yourself why you think it's okay to be dishonest. Then ask God to help you to become a more honest person.

31–50 = Disingenuous Deceiver. Your HQ is pretty low. You think that little white lies and situational ethics are acceptable, but you are only fooling yourself and others. Ask God to teach you to speak the truth in love.

51–75 = Rash Rationalizer. Your HQ is unimpressive. Maybe it's because you think others will like you better if you're not completely honest. Ask God to help you to accept yourself and to start being truthful with others.

76–120 = Mostly Honest. Your HQ is pretty good. Okay, you're not perfect, but who is? The good news is that you are sincere and really trying. Ask God to help you to keep it up!

121–150 = Too Good to Be True? Your HQ is questionable. Were you really honest in this quiz, or just trying to look good? Ask God to reveal the real truth to you.

Unlimited Credit Limit

Wouldn't it be nice if we only blew it once and only had to be forgiven once? Yeah, in your dreams! Real people in real life make mistakes all the time—and that means you need to bring them to God all the time too.

Fortunately, God doesn't have a "credit limit" on how many times he is willing to forgive you. In fact, when Peter asked Jesus how many times he should forgive someone who offended him (Matthew 18:21-22), Jesus told him to forgive his friend "seventy times seven" times. So, what does that really mean? Did Jesus want the man to forgive someone 490 times? And then what?

Some scholars believe that since the number seven is considered a perfect number and that seven times seven would symbolize infinity. And "seventy times seven" would be like infinity times ten—or in other words, infinity times infinity—and that is way more times than anyone can even count. That suggests that we can never wear out God's grace—he will always forgive us, clear into infinity.

Ask Yourself . . .

10. How often do I estimate I sin during the course of one day? Whether it's a bad thought, dishonesty, saying something unkind, or ignoring someone—how often do I blow it? (Be honest.)

11. How often do I confess these sins to God? Does the number of times I blow it equal the number of times I'm coming to God? Why or why not?

12. On a scale of 1 to 10, how do I think God would rate my honest spontaneity when it comes to promptly confessing my sins to him?

   1 = Barely moving, slower than a snail stuck in molasses

   5 = Slow but steady, as quick as a motivated tortoise

   10 = No time to waste, faster than a hungry hawk

   Why do I think I deserve that rating?

More Is More

"Two men were in debt to a banker.

One owed five hundred silver pieces, the other fifty.

Neither of them could pay up, and so the banker canceled both debts.

Which of the two would be more grateful?"

Simon answered, "I suppose the one who was forgiven the most."

"That's right," said Jesus.

Luke 7:41-43

13. Luke 7:42 states that whoever is forgiven the most will normally be the most thankful. What are the implications of that?

14. Should you blow it more often just so that you can be forgiven more times? Why or why not?

15. Maybe you think you're doing okay and you don't really need that much forgiveness. How does that affect the amount of time and energy you put into loving God?

16. Or maybe you realize you blow a lot. Does knowing how great it will feel to be forgiven make it easier for you to come back to God? Why or why not?

Words to Live By

(Consider memorizing one of these.)

Take a hard look at my life of hard labor,

Then lift this ton of sin.

Psalm 25:18

I remind you, my dear children:

Your sins are forgiven in Jesus' name.

1 John 2:12

Journal Your Thoughts

Choose one of the verses above. Write below what those words mean to you.

My Goal

Now you see how God's plan for forgiveness comes in the form of his Son Jesus Christ. But what does that mean to you personally? Write at least one goal about how you plan to implement Jesus' forgiveness to you. (Examples: *I want to be more honest in my prayers. I see the need to confess my sins more often.*)

My Goal(s):

My Prayer

Use this space to write a prayer about God's forgiveness. It can be a thank-you prayer or a request for help in a specific area.

He doesn't treat us as our sins deserve,

nor pay us back in full for our wrongs.

As high as heaven is over the earth,

so strong is his love to those who fear him.

And as far as sunrise is from sunset,

he has separated us from our sins.

Psalm 103:10-12

forgiving others

Be gentle with one another, sensitive.
Forgive one another as quickly and thoroughly
as God in Christ forgave you.

Ephesians 4:32

So you're beginning to understand the power of forgiveness in your own life now. You are experiencing firsthand what a relief it is to be forgiven not just once or twice, but on a continual (seventy times seven) basis—and by God, the King of the Universe. And what does God ask in return? Simply that you forgive others.

Sounds simple enough, doesn't it? Until you consider how many people ruin their own lives by totally ignoring this powerful principle. If you were to interview hundreds of people—people living miserable lives (with ruined marriages, failed careers, addiction problems, prison sentences) you'd probably discover that 99 percent of them had refused to forgive someone from their past. You'd see that these unhappy people were living in a constant state of bitterness and blame. To them it's always someone else's fault that their lives turned out so badly. But until they make a choice to forgive those who have hurt them and take responsibility for their own actions and choices, they will never escape their miserable rut of self-defeat. That's the power of unforgiveness—it essentially puts you into prison.

But God doesn't want you stuck in that kind of a prison. And even more than that, God doesn't want you to disconnect yourself from him by refusing to forgive someone else. And that's essentially what happens when you refuse to forgive. Not only do you wind up miserable but you lose out on God's mercy and forgiveness as well. In other words, it's a real lose-lose situation.

Stay Connected

In prayer there is a connection between
what God does and what you do.
You can't get forgiveness from God, for instance,
without also forgiving others.
If you refuse to do your part, you cut yourself off from God's part.
Matthew 6:14-15

1. Think about a time when someone deeply hurt you. Describe how you felt toward this person right at that very moment.

2. What did you do (if anything) to deal with the situation? Did you forgive the person? Why or why not?

3. How do you feel about this person right now? Why?

Hypocrisy's Reward

Remember when Jesus told Peter he had to forgive seventy times seven times? Well this is the story Jesus told his disciples after that:

> The kingdom of God is like a king who decided to square accounts with his servants. As he got under way, one servant was brought before him who had run up a debt of a hundred thousand dollars. He couldn't pay up, so the king ordered the man, along with his wife, children, and goods, to be auctioned off at the slave market.
>
> The poor wretch threw himself at the king's feet and begged, "Give me a chance and I'll pay it all back." Touched by his plea, the king let him off, erasing the debt.

The servant was no sooner out of the room when he came upon one of his fellow servants who owed him ten dollars. He seized him by the throat and demanded, "Pay up. Now!"

The poor wretch threw himself down and begged, "Give me a chance and I'll pay it all back." But he wouldn't do it. He had him arrested and put in jail until the debt was paid. When the other servants saw this going on, they were outraged and brought a detailed report to the king.

The king summoned the man and said, "You evil servant! I forgave your entire debt when you begged me for mercy. Shouldn't you be compelled to be merciful to your fellow servant who asked for mercy?" The king was furious and put the screws to the man until he paid back his entire debt. And that's exactly what my Father in heaven is going to do to each one of you who doesn't forgive unconditionally anyone who asks for mercy. (Matthew 18:23-35)

What's Up with This?

4. So what's Jesus' point in this story?

5. Why do you think the guy who'd been forgiven was so unforgiving?

"Be alert. If you see your friend going wrong, correct him.
If he responds, forgive him.
Even if it's personal against you and repeated seven times through the day,
and seven times he says, 'I'm sorry, I won't do it again,' forgive him."

Luke 17:3-4

the forgiving scale

Let's see where you rank on the Forgiving Scale. How do you think you would react in these hypothetical situations? Circle A, B, or C.

1. A girl at school starts spreading an untrue rumor about me so I:
   (A) take a couple of friends and confront her and demand that she take it back
   (B) talk to her and ask her why she's doing this
   (C) say nothing and pretend like I don't care

2. My PE teacher knows I'm deathly afraid of heights but insists I'm first up on the high balance beam, so I:
   (A) tell her off in front of everyone
   (B) discreetly ask her to rethink her decision
   (C) keep my mouth shut and force myself onto the beam

3. My best friend told her boyfriend my biggest secret, and now I'll:
   (A) never speak to her again
   (B) tell her she hurt me and ask her why she did it
   (C) say, "It's okay, but please don't do it again"

4. I'm late meeting a friend at the mall, and she's seriously ticked, so I:
   (A) tell her to lighten up since she's been late before
   (B) say I'm really sorry and try to change the subject
   (C) apologize several times then offer to buy her a soda

5. My mom said I could use her car, then changed her mind, so I:
   (A) storm off to my room
   (B) ask her if I can use it later
   (C) tell her "no problem" and forget about it

6. A friend says my outfit makes me look a little fat, so I:
   (A) let her know what I think about her outfit
   (B) shrug it off and forget about it
   (C) thank her for her honesty and never wear that outfit again

7. My sister borrows my new jeans but "forgets" to return them, so I:
   (A) go get them back myself as well as a couple of her things
   (B) ask her why she hasn't returned them
   (C) forget about it and hope she returns them eventually

8. A good friend is making the move on my major crush, so I:
   (A) tell her to back off or be sorry
   (B) ask her if she knows that I like him
   (C) pretend like I don't care

9. My dad promised to pick me up after youth group and then forgot, so I:
   (A) beg a ride from a friend and then go home and yell at him
   (B) call him to ask if he's coming
   (C) walk home alone even though it's dark

10. My algebra teacher wrongly accuses me of cheating on a test, so I:
    (A) deny it, make a scene, and storm out
    (B) ask him why he thinks that and attempt to explain my innocence
    (C) take the heat and the punishment without speaking

Scoring system: A = 3 points, B = 5 points, C = 8 points

   30–35 points = **Tough Chick.** People better watch out when they mess with you. The problem is, you're really hurting yourself by taking it out on others. Watch out.

   36–49 points = **Whatever Chick.** You think you're pretty laid back and able to show your feelings, but you're not really showing much grace or forgiveness. Lighten up.

   50–69 points = **Gracious Girl.** You're being fairly honest and straightforward, and trying to do it in love. You put yourself in a good place to forgive others. Way to go!

   70–80 points = **Pushover Girl.** Sure, you might *think* you're forgiving everyone, but you might just be pretending and repressing so that you'll look good. Take a second look.

"And when you assume the posture of prayer,
remember that it's not all asking.
If you have anything against someone, forgive—
only then will your heavenly Father be inclined
to also wipe your slate clean of sins."

Mark 11:25

maggie's story continues

After I call Dad and he agrees to meet me for coffee this afternoon, I briefly consider calling my mom to let her know that I'm at Claire's. Maybe I could even tell her that I'm planning to meet Dad for coffee, but then I wonder, why bother? Why not give her some time to stew on this; maybe she'll reconsider this whole thing and actually feel bad and take some responsibility for the annihilation of her marriage and our family! So I don't call. And when my caller ID says that she's trying to reach me on my cell, I don't pick up. I think she deserves this.

Finally, it's almost two. I arrive at Starbucks before Dad does, order my mocha, and find a quiet table in the corner. My dad finally arrives at about 2:15. Okay, he's never been a very punctual guy. So I let him buy me another mocha and we sit down to talk.

"You've heard the news?" he asks with the most dismal expression imaginable.

I nod. "Yeah. Mom told me this morning. And it totally sucks."

He doesn't say anything, just blows the steam off his Americana.

"Well, if it makes you feel any better, I'm on your side, Dad."

He looks up, kind of surprised like, then frowns. "Did your mom tell you everything, Maggie?"

"Just that you had moved out and were staying with Gary until you get your own place."

"Did she tell you why?"

I roll my eyes. "Well, I assume it's because Mom finally drove you crazy with all her nagging and yipping. Who could blame you, Dad? It's like she's turned into witch woman — I don't even know how you could stand it these past few months."

He doesn't say anything, and it occurs to me that he, unlike Mom, doesn't want to speak badly of his spouse. Very honorable. Well, sorry, but I'm not that mature. "The truth is, I'm sick of her too, Dad," I confess. "In fact, I'm thinking that maybe, when you get your own place, well, maybe I could come live with you."

"Oh, Maggie . . ."

Now I can't tell if he's pleased or worried. "I mean, if you want me to," I say quickly. "I could cook and clean and stuff."

"I know you could . . . that's not it."

I pause to study him. He looks like he's in serious turmoil. "Oh," I say suddenly, "are you thinking about coming home? Do you want to try to patch things up with Mom?" Now, even as I say this, I'm thinking no way. But who knows?

"No . . . that's not going to happen."

"How can you be so sure? I mean, what if Mom changed? What if she started acting like her old self again? Maybe there are pills she can take? Or maybe she's fallen away from God and needs to — "

"That's not the problem, Maggie."

"Oh."

"It's complicated."

I make an exasperated sigh now. "Look, Dad, I might only be sixteen, but I think I can handle 'complicated.' What are you trying to say anyway? I mean, if it's bad about Mom, I can take it. I'm pretty fed up with her too."

"It's not your mom's fault."

"Huh?" Now, I realize he's being pretty gracious toward Mom, but he doesn't need to cover for her.

"It's me, Maggie. I'm the one who messed up."

"What are you saying?"

He looks down at his coffee and fiddles with the stirring stick.

"What?" I say again, losing my patience.

He looks up now and I swear I have never seen my dad look so sad and serious. I mean, I think he was about to cry. And this just broke my heart. "What is it?" I say for the third time. "What's going on?"

"I've, uh, been seeing someone . . ."

"What do you mean?"

"I'm involved with someone . . . a woman . . ."

"You mean, as in an affair?"

Then he slowly nods without really looking at me. Now if he'd reached across the table and slapped me across the face, I couldn't have been more surprised. My dad, the guy who always made sure we were up in time to get to church, the leader of his men's fellowship group, a member of Promise Keepers, was having an affair?

"No," I say slowly, thinking I must've misunderstood.

He nods again, very soberly. "I'm sorry, Maggie, and I can't even begin to tell you how hard it is to — "

"You are having an affair?"

He glances around the room, as if he's worried that someone might *hear me, then speaks quietly. "Yes. I am having an affair."*

"Meaning you are cheating on Mom?" I'm still trying to take this in, trying to wrap my confused little mind around this staggering concept.

"Call it what you like, Maggie. And I know it's wrong. But I couldn't help myself — Lenora and I just fell in love."

"Lenora?" I say with even more disbelief. "Not as in Mom's good friend Lenora Hampton, worship leader at our church?"

He nods with his eyes downcast.

Now this is making me really sick. I mean seriously ill. Like I am going to hurl all over this little round table. Instead I just stand up and walk out. By the time I get outside it's like the whole world is spinning around and I don't know if I can even stand up straight. I head for my car, get in, lock the doors, and call Claire. "Help!" I yell when she answers.

"What?" she cries out. "Maggie, is that you? What's wrong?"

"Help me!" And then I just start sobbing.

6. Maggie has been blaming her mom for the fact their family is falling apart. But now she has learned something that changes things. How do you think she's feeling right now?

7. If you were Maggie's friend, what would you say to her?

8. If you were Maggie, what would you want someone to say to you?

What Comes Around . . .

"Don't pick on people, jump on their failures, criticize their faults—
unless, of course, you want the same treatment.
Don't condemn those who are down; that hardness can boomerang.
Be easy on people; you'll find life a lot easier.
Give away your life; you'll find life given back,
but not merely given back—given back with bonus and blessing.
Giving, not getting, is the way.
Generosity begets generosity."

Luke 6:37-38

Jesus taught again and again about certain things—specifically, things like forgiving and not judging others. Often he would make the same point over and over but in the form of different stories—just so his listeners would get it. That's how much he believed in these concepts. In fact, he believed in them so much that he gave up his life for them—just to make a point.

Luke 6:37-38 makes it very clear that you will receive the same kind of treatment you give. Oh, it might not happen on the same day, but eventually your behavior will catch up with you. If you treat others with kindness and forgiveness and generosity, it will eventually come back to you. What goes around really does come around, and Jesus understood this. But if you hold grudges and refuse to forgive others, you will eventually be backed into a corner where forgiveness will be withheld from you too. Jesus does not want you to go there.

What About You?

9. Describe a time when you held a grudge against someone (even for just a day).

10. How did you feel as a result of holding a grudge?

11. How do you think God felt about you while you were holding a grudge?

So if you forgive him, I forgive him.
Don't think I'm carrying around a list of personal grudges.
The fact is that I'm joining in with your forgiveness,
as Christ is with us, guiding us.
After all, we don't want to unwittingly give Satan
an opening for yet more mischief—
we're not oblivious to his sly ways!

2 Corinthians 2:10-11

What About Holding a Grudge for a Friend?

Occasionally, someone you really care about will get hurt, and as a result their pain will pull you in. Say your best friend's jerk of a boyfriend breaks her heart, and you're so furious that you want to knock his lights out. Sure, God wants you to feel empathy for your friend, and he wants you to listen, care about, and support her. But he does *not* want you to take up her offense. No matter how tempting it is to fight your friend's battles or to hate your friend's enemies, this is not what God wants from you.

Don't be fooled—holding a grudge for a friend is no different from holding a grudge for yourself. The best way you can encourage your friend is to help her to forgive the "jerk" who broke her heart, to learn from the pain, and then move on. Clinging to the pain and hanging onto the grudge will only disable her and make it hurt more in the long run.

Laugh with your happy friends when they're happy;
share tears when they're down.

Romans 12:15

Ask Yourself . . .

12. Have I ever taken up an offense for a friend? If so, describe the situation.

13. In the long run, how do I think my grudge helped or hindered the situation?

14. What's the best way a friend can help you to move on (instead of holding onto a grudge)?

Your New Designer Outfit

So, chosen by God for this new life of love,
dress in the wardrobe God picked out for you:
compassion, kindness, humility, quiet strength, discipline.
Be even-tempered, content with second place, quick to forgive an offense.
Forgive as quickly and completely as the Master forgave you.
And regardless of what else you put on, wear love.
It's your basic, all-purpose garment. Never be without it.

Colossians 3:12-14

What Not to Wear

Maybe you've seen that show where the style experts seek out unsuspecting, hard-working, fashion-challenged victims and secretly videotape them wearing some of their worst outfits. Seriously, some of these poor style offenders have been taped in their stretched-out, faded, and torn underwear. Now that's some pathetic reality TV.

But what if the roles were reversed? What if the fashion experts were secretly filmed in regard to their "character clothes"? Meaning, what if viewers got to watch them being mean-spirited, unforgiving, judgmental, or unkind? How would they look then? Okay, maybe that's as pathetic as their show, but the point is, God wants you to go around wearing his designer outfit (as described in Colossians 3:12-14). He knows you'll look totally awesome when you're dressed in compassion and kindness and all those other beautiful qualities—and of course, always wear love. It's your best look!

Words to Live By

(Consider memorizing this verse.)

Keep us forgiven with you and forgiving others.

Matthew 6:12

Journal Your Thoughts

That's a pretty short verse, but it gets to the point. Write about what it means to you.

My Goal

What has meant the most to you in this chapter about forgiving others? Think of at least one goal that will challenge you throughout the upcoming week.

My Goal(s):

My Prayer

Now take some time to write a prayer, asking God to help you attain your goal and to get a better grasp on why you need to practice forgiving others on a regular basis.

Because of the sacrifice of the Messiah,

his blood poured out on the altar of the Cross,

we're a free people—

free of penalties and punishments chalked up by all our misdeeds.

And not just barely free, either.

Abundantly free!

Ephesians 1:7

forgiving yourself

Then I let it all out;

I said, "I'll make a clean breast of my failures to GOD."

Suddenly the pressure was gone—

my guilt dissolved,

my sin disappeared.

Psalm 32:5

Do you ever get the feeling that you've done something so bad, so horrific and so evil, that even God won't forgive you? If so, you're not alone. Most people feel like this at some point in time. But do you think it's God who makes you feel like that? No way! God is all about forgiveness—forgiveness is the reason he allowed his beloved Son to be killed on the cross.

Satan is the one who wants you to feel like a total loser, like God can't or won't forgive you, and it's a big fat lie! So don't give in to it. If you do, you are saying that what Jesus did on the cross was insufficient. You are implying that God's grace is not enough. And really, you don't want to go there.

Now as important as the previous chapter was (on forgiving others) this is equally important, because the fact is, if you refuse to forgive yourself, it's going to seriously impact whether or not you can forgive others. Forgiving is a lot like love—if you can't love yourself, you can't love others.

> "Love others as well as you love yourself."
> Matthew 22:39

A Man in Need of Grace

David was a man with fantastic potential, a man "after God's own heart," but also a man who was known to blow it occasionally. Did you know that when David was king he plotted to have a man murdered after he'd slept with the man's wife? Pretty nasty stuff. And yet God did forgive him—eventually. Anyway, here is a psalm that David wrote about being forgiven. When you read it, imagine that you are saying these words to God.

> O my soul, bless GOD.
> From head to toe, I'll bless his holy name!
> O my soul, bless GOD,
> don't forget a single blessing!
> He forgives your sins—every one.
> He heals your diseases—every one.
> He redeems you from hell—saves your life!
> He crowns you with love and mercy—a paradise crown.
> He wraps you in goodness—beauty eternal.
> He renews your youth—you're always young in his presence.

GOD makes everything come out right;

he puts victims back on their feet.

He showed Moses how he went about his work,

opened up his plans to all Israel.

GOD is sheer mercy and grace;

not easily angered, he's rich in love.

He doesn't endlessly nag and scold,

nor hold grudges forever.

He doesn't treat us as our sins deserve,

nor pay us back in full for our wrongs.

As high as heaven is over the earth,

so strong is his love to those who fear him.

And as far as sunrise is from sunset,

he has separated us from our sins.

As parents feel for their children,

GOD feels for those who fear him.

He knows us inside and out,

keeps in mind that we're made of mud.

Men and women don't live very long;

like wildflowers they spring up and blossom,

But a storm snuffs them out just as quickly,

leaving nothing to show they were here.

GOD's love, though, is ever and always,

eternally present to all who fear him,

Making everything right for them and their children

as they follow his Covenant ways

and remember to do whatever he said.

GOD has set his throne in heaven;

he rules over us all. He's the King!

So bless GOD, you angels,

ready and able to fly at his bidding,

quick to hear and do what he says.

Bless GOD, all you armies of angels,

alert to respond to whatever he wills.

Bless GOD, all creatures, wherever you are—

everything and everyone made by GOD.

And you, o my soul, bless GOD!

Psalm 103:1-22

What About This?

1. Do you think there's anything you've done that God does not want to forgive you for? If so, what?

2. If God has forgiven others for murder, rape, stealing, arson, assault—what could you have done that is so unforgivable?

3. Have you ever confessed this sin to God? Why or why not?

A Little Help from Your Friends . . .

If you're having a hard time forgiving yourself, it may be that you need some help. That's where Christian friends and fellowship come into play. God wants you to be in a position—whether it's a Bible study, youth group, some form of Christian fellowship—where you can be encouraged and supported by trusted believers.

God wants you to have people in your life you can turn to when you're feeling down. This is especially true if you're unable to forgive yourself. In James 5:15-16 you are encouraged to "confess your sins to each other." Now this isn't so that you can be shocking or sensational. And it's not a place to gather gossip tidbits to spread around at school. It's a safe haven where you and your Christian friends can be honest and open, trusting each other and praying for each other in order for healing to occur.

God knows that you can't make it alone—and this is just one area when he wants you to be hooked up with a trusted group of Christian friends.

Believing-prayer will heal you, and Jesus will put you on your feet.
And if you've sinned, you'll be forgiven—healed inside and out.
Make this your common practice:

Confess your sins to each other
and pray for each other so that you can live together whole and healed.
The prayer of a person living right with God
is something powerful to be reckoned with.
James 5:15-16

What About You?

4. Are you participating in some sort of fellowship where you feel
   safe enough to confess your sins and ask for prayer? Or perhaps
   you could do this with just a couple of close and trusted friends.
   Describe how you might go about this.

5. Now, considering how you answered question 4, is there anything
   you'd like to see change in regard to your fellowship situation? If
   so, what?

6. If there is something you'd like to change in regard to your fellowship, how do you plan to be involved in this change? What role would you play?

maggie's story continues

After I talk to Claire briefly on the phone, she encourages me to come over and just chill for a while. Even so, I am still in a state of dumbfounded shock when I walk into her house.

"I can't believe this," I say as I flop down on the couch in her family room. "I just cannot believe it!"

She just nods and looks sad. "I know, Maggie. It's hard to hear stuff like that—I mean about your own parents."

I realize, not for the first time, that Claire has been there, done that, but sometimes I kind of forget. Sometimes I think that she's just fine, that her life has always been like this—split between two homes, two parents—no big deal.

I sigh and lean my head back, wondering what I should do. "I was totally wrong about my mom," I admit.

"I know."

I sit up and look at her. "You know? As in you knew all along? Or you know because I just told you?"

She shrugs. "*I guess I sort of wondered. . . . I mean I remember how it went with my parents. My mom suddenly turned into the meanest mom on the block, and she was always ragging on my dad and us kids. And then it turned out that Dad was the one who brought the whole thing on. I mean, my mom's not like all innocent or anything, but Dad was the one who cheated on her.*"

"*You've never told me all this before.*"

"*No point.*"

I consider this, but at the same time feel guilty. Like was it because there was no point, or was it because I wasn't really willing to listen? Kind of like I've been treating my mom. "I better go," *I say suddenly.*

"*You going to talk to your mom?*"

I nod and stand. "Yeah. I can't believe how I treated her. The way I was so quick to blame her for everything."

"*You were just going by what you could see, Maggie.*"

"*You mean like the surface?*"

She kind of smiled. "I guess that's all you could see, huh?"

"*Yeah, I might as well be blind sometimes.*"

Then Claire hugs me. "I'll be praying for you, Maggie. Call me if you need to talk, okay?"

"*Thanks,*" *I tell her. "I will.*"

"*And,*" *she says as I open the door, "don't be too hard on yourself.*"

"*Yeah, right.*" *I just shake my head and go outside. All I can think is that I've been a total jerk to my mom. My poor mom! Here Dad is off having an affair — with her good friend Lenora! It makes me totally sick and there's no telling how Mom must be feeling right now. And there I go, telling her off, stomping out the door, and acting like a total moronic idiot. What is wrong with me anyway?*

All the way home I am raging. Raging at my dad and myself. We are both jerks. Okay, he's a bigger jerk than me, but I'm nothing to be proud of either. And Christians? Yeah, right! How can we even call ourselves Christians when we act like this? And what's going to happen when people at church hear about this? Man, I'm not sure that I'll even want to show my face there anymore. It's like our whole family has gone to hell in a handbasket in one fell swoop. Why, God? All I can think now is why, God? Why would you allow this to happen?

David's Cry for Help

Bend an ear, GOD; answer me.
I'm one miserable wretch!
Keep me safe—haven't I lived a good life?
Help your servant—I'm depending on you!
You're my God; have mercy on me.
I count on you from morning to night.
Give your servant a happy life;
I put myself in your hands!
You're well-known as good and forgiving,
bighearted to all who ask for help.
Pay attention, GOD, to my prayer;
bend down and listen to my cry for help.
Every time I'm in trouble I call on you,
confident that you'll answer.

Psalm 86:1-7

What About This?

7. Maggie has fallen into the depths of despair. So has David in Psalm 86. Both are calling out to God, but their cries are different. What's the difference?

8. What do you do when you reach the lowest places? Where do you go?

Who God Is

If you really believe that God is who he says he is—if you really believe that Jesus is the Son of God and that he died on the cross to remove your sins—then you must admit that *you need to forgive yourself.* Anything less is a complete denial of God's true nature and plan for your life.

If you think you're being contrite or humble by withholding forgiveness from yourself, you are totally deceived. There is nothing you can do to remove your sins on your own. You need to take those sins directly to God, confess them, and trust that he really is who he says he is—and then you need to accept his forgiveness and thank him for his mercy and grace.

Listen from your home in heaven, forgive and reward us:
reward each life and circumstance,
For you know each life from the inside,
(you're the only one with such inside knowledge!),
So they'll live before you in lifelong reverence and believing
obedience on this land you gave our ancestors.
2 Chronicles 6:30-31

Getting Honest

9. List God's qualities (good, kind, just, creative) in the order of most importance to you.

10. List some of your strengths.

11. List your weaknesses, and see how they compare to your strengths.

I Am Weak, but You Are Strong

You probably remember the words to the old childhood song "Jesus Loves Me."

> Jesus loves me, this I know
> For the Bible tells me so.
> Little ones to Him belong,
> We are weak, but He is strong.

And that's just how simple it is. Jesus does love you—the Bible confirms this. And if you've given him your heart, you belong to him. And here's the clincher—you are weak, but he is strong. This is especially true in the area of self-forgiveness. You can't do it without him. So why not ask.

Pure and Simple

I remind you, my dear children:
Your sins are forgiven in Jesus' name.

1 John 2:12

how forgivable are you?

Circle True or False next to each statement as it applies to you.

1. I'm usually able to laugh at myself.
   True   False

2. I'm good at sniffing out problems or flaws in others.
   True   False

3. I know I make mistakes, but I learn from them.
   True   False

4. My mom says that I'm "high maintenance."
   True   False

5. My siblings talk to me about their problems sometimes.
   True   False

6. I really need people to respect me.
   True   False

7. My friends say I'm pretty easygoing.
   True   False

8. I always have the best ideas.
   True   False

9. I do my best and try not to worry about the rest.
   True   False

10. I have high expectations for myself and others.
    True   False

11. I would rather be happy than always right.
    True   False

12. My siblings say that I pick on them sometimes.
    True   False

13. I enjoy listening to my friends.
    True   False

14. My friends say I'm a perfectionist.
    True   False

15. I like seeing others succeed.
    True   False

16. I have a hard time letting go of an old offense.
    True   False

17. I like hearing about other people's ideas and dreams.
    True   False

18. I don't like to admit to my own mistakes.

    True   False

19. I'm able to forgive and forget pretty easily.

    True   False

20. I want everyone to respect my opinion.

    True   False

Give yourself 5 points for every odd number (1, 3, 5 . . .) that you circled True.

Subtract 5 points for every even number (2, 4, 6 . . .) that you circled True.

-20–15 points = **Unforgivable.** Your pride sets you up to be unforgiven, both by yourself and others. Ask God to teach you patience, kindness, and humility.

20–30 points = **On the Fence.** You can't decide whether to forgive others or focus on yourself. Ask God to help you consider others more important than yourself.

35–50 points = **Forgivable.** You don't take yourself too seriously and are able to treat others with love and respect. Thank God and ask him to continue leading you along this way.

Words to Live By

(Consider memorizing this verse.)

I want you to know, my very dear friends,
that it is on account of this resurrected Jesus
that the forgiveness of your sins can be promised.

Acts 13:38

Journal Your Thoughts

Consider the verses in this chapter and choose the one that most challenges your thinking when it comes to forgiving yourself. Now write about how you want your life to be changed by this verse.

My Goal

Consider what you've just journaled about and see if you can transform that into a practical goal. (Example: *I will forgive myself for* _____ *every morning for the next week.*)

My Goal(s):

My Prayer

Now use this space to write a prayer, asking God to help you to meet your goal and to grow in the area of self-forgiveness.

Then [Jesus] spoke to her: "I forgive your sins."
That set the dinner guests talking behind his back:
"Who does he think he is, forgiving sins!"
He ignored them and said to the woman,
"Your faith has saved you. Go in peace."
Luke 7:48-50

forgiving the unforgivable

I'm telling you to love your enemies.

Let them bring out the best in you, not the worst.

When someone gives you a hard time,

respond with the energies of prayer,

for then you are working out of your true selves,

your God-created selves.

This is what God does.

He gives his best

—the sun to warm and the rain to nourish—

to everyone, regardless:

the good and bad, the nice and nasty.

Matthew 5:44-45

*E*veryone has, or will have, at least one "unforgivable" person in their life. And if you haven't come across that unfortunate person yet, it's likely that someday you will. For some people the unforgivable will come in the serious form of an abuser or even worse. It just happens.

So what do you do when someone hurts you in a way that seems totally unforgivable? How can you be expected to forgive something that's horrible, sinful, and perhaps even illegal? Maybe you wonder how that's even humanly possible? Well, the truth is, it's not.

Most of the time when you practice forgiveness, you need God's assistance. In the case of forgiving the unforgivable, you need God's divine intervention—because you can't do it alone. And yet, as you can see in Matthew 5:44-45, God not only encourages you to forgive these people, he expects it of you.

However, God does not necessarily expect you to accept this person's behavior, or to trust this person, or even to ever be involved with this person again. And in many cases he also doesn't expect you to understand why this person hurt you, or to think that what this person did to you was no big deal. It was a big deal. God knows that.

Does forgiving someone mean that the person who hurt you is off the hook? That he or she gets to simply walk free and never account for those sins? Not at all. Offenders are still accountable to God, and he will deal with them justly. And if they have broken the law, the legal system will deal with them as well. Forgiveness is simply God's method for beginning the healing that he wants to accomplish within you. It's his ticket to moving on with your life.

Loving the Useless

We can understand someone dying for a person worth dying for,
and we can understand how someone good and noble
could inspire us to selfless sacrifice.
But God put his love on the line for us by offering his Son in sacrificial death
while we were of no use whatever to him.

Romans 5:7-8

What About You?

1. According to Romans 5:7-8, is there anyone who is truly "unforgivable"? Why or why not?

2. Is there someone in your life you have difficulty forgiving? Explain why.

3. Why does it sometimes seem easier to not forgive someone? Is it because it feels good to be bitter and angry?

4. List three good reasons for you to forgive someone.

Double Whammy

Here's the thing: By refusing to forgive someone who has seriously hurt you, you not only experience the pain of the actual event but you continue to reexperience it again and again, all because you are unable to let it go. It's like you're allowing that person to continually hurt you—over and over. Forgiveness is your exit plan from the pain. Sure, it's not always a one-stop deal where you forgive and forget and that's it. But it's the first step in the beginning of healing.

Next Step

Now we look inside, and what we see is that
anyone united with the Messiah
gets a fresh start, is created new.
The old life is gone; a new life burgeons!
Look at it!
All this comes from the God who settled the
relationship between us and him,
and then called us to settle our
relationships with each other.
2 Corinthians 5:17-18

What Do You Think?

5. Why do you think God wants you to forgive someone who doesn't deserve your forgiveness?

6. Second Corinthians 5:17-18 says God calls us "to settle our relationships with each other." What does that mean to you?

7. Do you think forgiveness should have limits? Why or why not?

maggie's story continues

When I get home, I can't find my mom anywhere. Her car is in the driveway, so I'm sure she must be here. I just don't know where. After searching the house, I am feeling frantic and worried and a little bit scared. What could've happened to her? Where has she gone? I hope she hasn't done anything drastic. Finally, I go out on the deck and call out her name.

"Maggie?" I hear Mom's voice coming from somewhere in our backyard.

I walk around the deck to see my mom over in a corner of the yard. She is on her knees in what looks like a pile of dirt. "Mom!" I cry, running over to see if she's okay. "What are you doing?"

She holds up a spade. "I was trying to start a garden."

"A garden?"

She slowly stands up, wiping the dirt from her hands onto her already dirty overalls. "Yeah, I've always wanted to plant a garden."

I look at the freshly turned soil. "Did you do all that?"

"No. Susan next door had a guy over tilling her garden this morning, so I paid him to come over and do this little patch for me."

"A garden?" I repeat, trying to understand why my usually neat and tidy mom wants to come out here and root around in the dirt.

"Yeah. Your dad never wanted me to mess up the backyard . . ." She sighs deeply and gazes up at the sky. "But I thought maybe it was time for a change."

"I talked to Dad today," I tell her.

She looks back at me now, and I can tell she's curious. "And?"

"And he told me he's having an affair."

She sighs again, only this time it's tinged with relief.

"I'm sorry, Mom," I say, suddenly losing it again. "I'm sorry I blamed you — I was so wrong and I'm — "

But I don't get a chance to finish my apology because my mom grabs me into a big and somewhat earthy hug. "It's okay, sweetie," she assures me. "I just thought it would be best for you to hear it from your dad."

When I step away, Mom digs in her pocket to pull out a slightly dirty-looking tissue, but I use it to blow my nose anyway. "This totally sucks, Mom."

She nods. "I know. Want to talk about it?"

So we go sit on the deck, and she tells me that she suspected this for quite some time and finally found out the truth about a month ago. "At first I was so angry I couldn't even see straight," she tells me. "Then I thought we might be able to fix things . . . I thought maybe I could forgive your dad and we could start over."

"You could forgive him?" I say in a stunned voice.

"Well, not without God's help." She shakes her head sadly. "Even then, I wasn't so sure. But I was willing to go to marriage counseling and give it a try."

"So did you?"

She looks across the backyard, over to her little patch of dirt. "Your dad wasn't interested, Maggie."

"He's a total jerk!"

She doesn't say anything.

"I hate him!" I shout. "I will never speak to him again!"

"Maggie . . ."

"No, it's true. I really hate him, Mom. He's such a lying hypocrite. And Lenora too. She acts like she's so holy and good, standing up there leading worship — " I turn to Mom as realization hits me. "And she was *actually having an affair during the same time she was leading worship for the whole church?"*

Mom nods sadly. "Christians aren't perfect, Maggie. Just forgiven."

"Yeah, I've heard that one before," I say bitterly. "And maybe God can forgive Dad and Lenora, but it'll be snowing down below before I do."

"Oh, Maggie."

Now is the time to forgive this man and help him back on his feet. If all you do is pour on the guilt, you could very well drown him in it. My counsel now is to pour on the love.

2 Corinthians 2:7-8

What About You?

8. Maggie says she'll never forgive her dad. Have you ever felt like that toward someone? Describe how that feels.

9. Second Corinthians 2:7-8 says that you can drown a person in guilt. Describe how a person might actually do that to someone else.

God's Way

Matthew 5:46-48 says it's no big deal to love people who are lovable. Even the worst criminal can do that. But God set a higher example by loving you when you were at your very worst—meaning he loved you unconditionally, just the way you were. And he wants you to be able to do the same with others. In other words, he expects you to "grow up" and start doing things God's way instead of your own. That might mean reaching out to someone you don't like, forgiving someone who doesn't deserve it, or biting your tongue when you'd rather cut loose on someone who's being a jerk.

The thing is, you have to make a conscious choice to put aside your own agenda in order to embrace God's. But once you start making that choice, your life will start changing in miraculous ways. And you will look more like God.

"If all you do is love the lovable, do you expect a bonus?
Anybody can do that.
If you simply say hello to those who greet you, do you expect a medal?
Any run-of-the-mill sinner does that.
In a word, what I'm saying is, Grow up.
You're kingdom subjects. Now live like it.
Live out your God-created identity.
Live generously and graciously toward others,
the way God lives toward you.
Matthew 5:46-48

Getting Honest

10. Are you really willing to do things God's way when it comes to forgiveness? Why or why not?

11. Describe one specific situation or relationship where you know God is calling you to handle things differently.

12. What do you think it means to love and forgive *unconditionally*?

What If I Just Can't?

Okay, maybe you've gotten this far, but you are still stuck in the land of unforgiveness. What then? First of all, you need to admit your weakness to God. And remember God's promise in 2 Corinthians 12:9: "My grace is enough; it's all you need. My strength comes into its own in your weakness." This means that if you allow God, he can step in where you are incapable and empower you. But it might also mean that he'll lead you to another source of help as well. So if you find you are unable to get over this forgiveness hurdle on your own, invite God to lead you to the source that's right for you.

- A trusted family member who can help you to get the assistance you need

- Christian friends who can pray for and encourage you

- A trained counselor (from your church, school, or a private practice) who can guide you through the forgiving/healing process

- A self-help group that deals specifically with any of the heavier issues that make forgiveness difficult but necessary (abuse, rape, incest, and so on)

Or maybe you're assuming that *if* you forgive this unforgivable person, you'll have to get involved again. But that's not necessarily the case. If this person continues to hurt you or others, or proves untrustworthy, God expects you to keep a safe distance. Sure, you can and should care about and pray for this person, but you don't have to remain in a close relationship with him or her. And even if this person is a part of your life, you can still forgive as you maintain an emotional distance.

Ask Yourself . . .

13. Can I do this on my own? Or do I need to seek additional help? Why or why not?

14. What power will forgiving someone else have on my life?

A Blind Spot?

"If you enter your place of worship and, about to make an offering,
you suddenly remember a grudge a friend has against you,
abandon your offering, leave immediately,
go to this friend and make things right.
Then and only then, come back and work things out with God.
Or say you're out on the street and an old enemy accosts you.
Don't lose a minute. Make the first move; make things right with him.
After all, if you leave the first move to him, knowing his track record,
you're likely to end up in court, maybe even jail.
If that happens, you won't get out without a stiff fine."

Matthew 5:23-26

More Than One Side . . .

Often, if you look deep enough, you'll discover that forgiveness has two sides. Sure, you may assume that you're the only one who's been hurt in a particular situation, but you don't realize that you have a big blind spot. It's possible that you've done something that has wounded the one who in turn wounds you. This is often the case when two good friends suddenly become arch enemies. Both think that they are the victim, but in reality, they are both instigators. Even so, someone has to start the forgiveness wheels turning, so it might as well be you. Because, as Jesus says in Matthew 5:23-26, you need to work things out with your friends and enemies before you try to work things out with God.

Words to Live By

(Consider memorizing one of these.)

To you who are ready for the truth, I say this:
Love your enemies.
Let them bring out the best in you, not the worst.
Luke 6:27

When someone gives you a hard time,
respond with the energies of prayer for that person.
Luke 6:28

If someone slaps you in the face, stand there and take it.

If someone grabs your shirt,

giftwrap your best coat and make a present of it.

Luke 6:29

If someone takes unfair advantage of you,

use the occasion to practice the servant life.

No more tit-for-tat stuff.

Live generously.

Luke 6:30

Journal Your Thoughts

Choose one of the verses above. Write below what those words mean to you.

My Goal

What one thing really stands out to you in the area of forgiving the unforgivable? What do you think God is nudging you to do? Make your goal practical and doable.

My Goal(s):

My Prayer

Write a prayer inviting God to help you forgive. Or write a prayer for the person who has hurt you.

I tell you, love your enemies.

Help and give without expecting a return.

You'll never—I promise—regret it.

Live out this God-created identity the way our Father lives toward us,

generously and graciously,

even when we're at our worst.

Our Father is kind;

you be kind.

Luke 6:35-36

ministry of
reconciliation

God put the world square with himself through the Messiah,

giving the world a fresh start by offering forgiveness of sins.

God has given us the task of telling everyone what he is doing.

We're Christ's representatives.

God uses us to persuade men and women to drop their differences

and enter into God's work of making things right between them.

We're speaking for Christ himself now:

Become friends with God;

he's already a friend with you.

2 Corinthians 5:19-20

Christ's Reps

The final link in the forgiveness chain is the "ministry of reconciliation." And while that may sound like a mouthful, it's really pretty simple. Once you are walking with God and growing up, God will use you to draw others to himself. Does this mean you must go out "recruiting" or "evangelizing" or "proselytizing" or "converting" others to

Christianity? Not necessarily. What it does mean is that God's love and mercy will become so evident in your life that others will be attracted to God because of it.

So instead of focusing on some numbers-driven door-to-door crusade (which God may or may not call you to do), you can focus your heart on having a solid relationship with God. And as you spend time with God, practicing a lifestyle that's driven by love and forgiveness, you will become a person whom others appreciate and trust—and, as a result, people will come to you.

Jesus Calls You to . . .

"Open the eyes of the outsiders
so they can see the difference between dark and light, and choose light,
see the difference between Satan and God, and choose God.
I'm sending you off to present my offer of sins forgiven,
and a place in the family,
inviting them into the company of those who begin real living
by believing in me."

Acts 26:18

What About This?

1. Can you see yourself as Jesus' representative? Why or why not?

2. What are some things that people might see in you that would draw them to God?

3. What are some things that people might see in you that would send them running the other direction?

Big Responsibility

Okay, it would be easy to get overwhelmed if you thought God was totally dependant on you to get his Word out. Like what if you blow it? Or have a bad day? Or simply forget to let your "little light shine"? The bad news is that all of those things will probably happen to you, but the good news is that God can use all of it. Because, more than anything else, God wants you to have an honest and willing heart—and if you blow it, just confess it, say I'm sorry, and move on. No big deal.

You see, your biggest responsibility is to remain hooked up with God. And that's because he wants to do his work *through* you—not the other way around. And that means being available, ready, and willing. It doesn't mean being perfect, having the Bible memorized, or being able to speak "Christianese" (which is really an antiquated man-made language that is best left behind).

Love Speaks Louder Than Words

Watch what God does, and then you do it,

like children who learn proper behavior from their parents.

Mostly what God does is love you.

Keep company with him and learn a life of love.

Observe how Christ loved us.

His love was not cautious but extravagant.

He didn't love in order to get something from us

but to give everything of himself to us.

Love like that.

Ephesians 5:1-2

4. Describe someone you consider to be a "mature" Christian.

5. List ten Christlike character qualities that you'd like to be visible in your life.

6. Now, if you only had two of those qualities—which would you choose?

maggie's story ends . . .

Two totally miserable weeks have passed since I heard about my dad's affair. Of course, the church knows all about it by now. Lenora has "stepped down" as the esteemed worship leader, and both she and Dad no longer attend there anymore. What a relief!

To my surprise, both Mom and I have been totally accepted and treated well at church. Okay, I know there's a lot of pity going on, but under the circumstances, I guess it's understandable.

I haven't spoken to Dad once. I don't take his calls, and I don't respond to the messages he leaves. In fact, I'm considering having his number blocked from my cell phone. That should send a message!

But here's what gets me—I heard that Dad and Lenora are not only still together, but they've started going to a church on the other side of town. What's up with that? And it's like the idea of them sitting there in church, acting like they're perfectly fine, is just eating me alive. It's like I can literally feel my stomach chewing on itself. Seriously, I've been having these really bad stomachaches.

"I think I need to go to the doctor," I finally tell Mom as I help her weed her garden, which is really looking pretty good. When she asks me why, I explain how my stomach hurts all the time. "Do you think I have an ulcer?" I ask.

"I guess it's possible." She frowns as she tosses out a weed. "But do you know what can really irritate an ulcer, Maggie?"

I shrug. "Stomach acid?"

"Yes. But do you know that stress and worry can create stomach acid?"

"Yeah, I guess . . ."

"You need to forgive your dad, Maggie."

I don't say anything. The truth is, both Claire and our youth pastor have told me the same thing. Not only that, but there's this little God-voice that's starting to get louder, and it's saying the same thing.

"I know it's hard, Maggie. And I sure couldn't do it without God's help."

"So you've really forgiven him?"

"It's kind of a daily thing. And sometimes it's about a hundred times in one day."

"But you're doing it?"

"If I don't, I'll probably have an ulcer too. That and high blood pressure and God only knows what else. It took me a while to figure it out, but I know that not forgiving him mostly punishes me. And I don't need any more grief."

I nod and stand up straight. "I think you're right."

"God will help you, Maggie. If you ask him."

So I go inside my room, close the door, get down on my knees, and I ask God to help me to forgive my dad. And even though I don't feel very forgiving, I say the words. "I forgive my dad, God. But I need your help to really mean it." And I say a few more things and finally I get up and feel just a tiny bit better.

Okay, I know this is going to take time, and like Mom says, I might need to forgive him a hundred times a day. But I guess that's all I can *do for now. And maybe, if God does an extreme miracle, maybe I'll actually be able to talk to him again someday. But not today. All I can do today, with God's help, is to forgive him. But at least I can do that. That's something. Who knows what will happen on down the line?*

Reconciled and Reunited . . .

Christ brought us together through his death on the Cross.
The Cross got us to embrace, and that was the end of the hostility.
Christ came and preached peace to you outsiders
and peace to us insiders.
He treated us as equals, and so made us equals.
Through him we both share the same Spirit and have
equal access to the Father.

Ephesians 2:16-18

What About You?

7. Maggie finally came to the place where she is ready to forgive her dad. Do you think she could've reached this place sooner? Why or why not?

8. How do you think the rest of Maggie's story will go? Will she ever reconcile with her dad?

They're Watching

Do you realize that you're being watched? It's quite likely that, if people know you're a Christian, you are being observed. Now this shouldn't make you nervous, because it's actually part of God's plan. He wants others to see you up close and personal—he wants them to observe your life, your faith, your love, and your forgiveness *in action*. That means the next time some girl in PE makes a snide remark to you, you can take it in stride, practice forgiveness, and repay the insult with love. Too much to expect? Maybe on your own, but not with God working in you.

You might be amazed to know how many people have turned to God after witnessing a Christian's love and grace in action. It's truly life changing!

A Better Way

"You're blessed when you can show people
how to cooperate instead of compete or fight.
That's when you discover who you really are,
and your place in God's family."

Matthew 5:9

Matthew 5:9 shows how important cooperation is—much better than competing or fighting. In fact, other versions of the Bible call this being a "peacemaker."

9. So what kind of peacemaker are you? On a scale of 1 to 10, where do you stand?

1   2   3   4   5   6   7   8   9   10

I enjoy a good fight.   I go out of my way to help others get along.

10. Describe what you think people see when they observe you interacting with others.

11. What would you like them to see?

what kind of reconciler are you?

Read the following statements and put whichever letter best represents how much you do these things in the box provided. Be honest.
Answers N = Never, S = Sometimes, O = Often, A = Always

1. ☐ I consider God to be my best friend.

2. ☐ I can sense when someone is hurting, and I try to reach out to that person.

3. ☐ I do what I can to encourage my friends.

4. ☐ I ask God to lead me throughout my day.

5. ☐ If my friends get into a disagreement, I try to break it up.

6. ☐ If someone offends me, I make the first move toward forgiveness.

7. ☐ I try to think more highly of others than I do of myself.

8. ☐ I do all I can to stay connected to God.

9. ☐ I try to find the positive side of a negative situation.

10. ☐ I go out of my way to smile or say hello to people I don't know.

11. ☐ I make a daily effort to have a quiet time with God.

12. ☐ Even if everyone is complaining, I try not to grumble.

13. ☐ I try to find the best in people.

14. ☐ I look for opportunities to help others.

15. ☐ I set aside time to read my Bible on a regular basis.

16. ☐ I am always asking God to make his love evident in my life.

17. ☐ I am committed to a fellowship group.

18. ☐ I contribute when I'm in fellowship group.

19. ☐ I am open to God leading me in new directions.

20. ☐ Nothing makes me happier than seeing God's light shine through me.

Now add up your score. N = 0 points, S = 5 points, O = 10 points, A = 15 points

0–50 points = **Resistant Reconciler.** You need some serious reconciliation yourself!

51–100 points = **Reluctant Reconciler.** You're trying, but have room for improvement.

101–200 points = **Reforming Reconciler.** You're on your way to becoming a real reconciler.

201–300 points = **Real Reconciler.** You're seriously committed to reconciliation!

The Cross Unites

Christ brought us together thro\ugh his death on the Cross.
The Cross got us to embrace, and that was the end of the hostility.
Christ came and preached peace to you
outsiders and peace to us insiders.
He treated us as equals, and so made us equals.
Through him we both share the same Spirit and
have equal access to the Father.

Ephesians 2:16-18

Words to Live By

(Consider memorizing this.)

"Master, listen to us!
Master, forgive us!
Master, look at us and do something!
Master, don't put us off!
Your city and your people are named after you:
You have a stake in us!"

Daniel 9:19

Journal Your Thoughts

Choose one of the verses from this chapter. Write below what those words mean to you.

My Goal

Now that you're almost finished with this book, prayerfully consider what goals you want to make in regard to forgiveness. Is it to be quicker to forgive yourself? To be more forgiving of others? To focus on becoming a better reconciler?

My Goal(s):

My Prayer

Pen a prayer to God. Maybe you'll ask him to help you understand reconciliation better, or you might invite him to reconcile others through your life. Just make sure the prayer is heartfelt and honest.

Not only that, but all the broken and dislocated pieces of the universe—
people and things, animals and atoms—
get properly fixed and fit together in vibrant harmonies,
all because of his death,
his blood that poured down from the Cross.

Colossians 1:20

author

*M*elody Carlson has written dozens of books for all age groups, but she particularly enjoys writing for teens. Perhaps this is because her own teen years remain so vivid in her memory. After claiming to be an atheist at the ripe old age of twelve, she later surrendered her heart to Jesus and has been following him ever since. Her hope and prayer for all her readers is that each one would be touched by God in a special way through her stories. For more information, visit Melody's website at www.melodycarlson.com.

DISCOVER A UNIQUE NEW KIND
OF BIBLE STUDY.

How did Jesus teach many of his most important lessons? He told stories. That's the idea behind the first series of Bible studies from best-selling fiction author Melody Carlson. In each of the four studies, Melody weaves fictional stories with practical discussion questions to get you thinking about some of the most important topics in life: your relationship with God, your relationship with others, identity, and forgiveness.

Finding Out Who You Really Are
1576837262

Making the Most of Your Relationships
1576837270

Knowing God Better Than Ever
1576837254

Visit your local Christian bookstore,
call NavPress at 1-800-366-7788, or log on to www.navpress.com to purchase.

To locate a Christian bookstore near you,
call 1-800-991-7747.

NAVPRESS
BRINGING TRUTH TO LIFE
www.navpress.com

TH1NK Books
an imprint of NavPress®